UNDER your FEET

written by
Jane Launchbury and Selma Montford

illustrated by Jane Launchbury

YOUNG LIBRARY

Be Streetwise

Towns are exciting places to explore, but they can be dangerous. All detectives need to be properly briefed and equipped.

Always tell an adult where you are going, how you are getting there, and when you expect to be back.

Wear a watch so you don't need to ask what the time is. Check opening times. Always let a parent know if you are delayed.

Take enough money for your return fare, and both change and a Phonecard for phone calls.

Don't talk to strangers. Before you go out, talk to an adult about who to ask for help in an emergency. (These may include police officers, traffic wardens, bus drivers, and post office, bank or station staff).

Keep your hand or foot against your belongings.

If you have a bicycle, learn how to use it safely.

Never play on building sites, on roads or on other people's property.

Try not to go out alone, and be home before dark.

Learn how to use a public phone, and how to make reverse charge and 999 calls.

Have an up-to-date map, and check transport timetables.

Never accept lifts or invitations into private buildings, even if you are very tired or lost.

Know the Green Cross Code. Read the Highway Code.

Always look where you are going. Don't walk along looking up at buildings, or step backwards into the road.

Never drop litter. Look for a bin or take it home with you.

Above all, use your common sense.

First published in 1990 by
YOUNG LIBRARY LTD
3 The Old Brushworks
56 Pickwick Road
Corsham, Wiltshire SN13 9BX

© Copyright 1990 Jane Launchbury and Selma Montford
All rights reserved

ISBN 1 85429 001 0

Printed and bound in Hong Kong

Contents

Undercover City	4
People at Work	6
Tunnels under Towns	8
Discovering Geology	10
Working in the Bowels of the Earth	12
Uncovering the Clues	14
Cellars, Shelters and Dungeons	16
Living in the Dark	18
Dead Bodies	20
The Sewers	22
Your own Model Town	24
Books to Read	26
Acknowledgements	26
Index	27

Undercover City

How well do you know your town? You probably think you can find your way about easily by knowing the roads, asking the way, and using a street map.

Here's a surprise for you. Imagine yourself in the centre of town. If you moved five or ten metres *in a certain direction* you would be utterly lost.

That direction is down!

There's another town beneath the one you know - a town few of us ever see. In this book we will take a look at it.

There are plenty of clues on the surface. You have probably tripped over the evidence many times!

Next time you walk along a street, look more closely at the ground. Set into the pavements and road surfaces you will see various shaped covers. Some have words on them, like 'water', 'gas' or 'Telecom'. Others just have raised patterns, which are sometimes very pretty.

Most of these covers are to allow workers to get at pipes and wires. Some cover shafts with a fixed ladder or rungs, for a person to climb down. Others, like the big trapdoors you see in pavements outside pubs, are for deliveries of goods. Drains have covers too, which are designed to let water through, but not twigs and rubbish.

In the days before modern heating, homes had open coal fires. The coal was often stored in a cellar beneath a pavement. The coalman delivered the coal through an opening in the pavement outside. You can see a picture of this on page 16.

See how many different types of covers you notice next time you are out. Try to find out or guess what each is for. These pictures may help you identify the various sorts.

Street drain cover

Coal-hole cover   *Water stopcock cover*

Glass cover which lets light into a basement

Grille which lets water and air to tree roots

4

Grating to let light and air into cellar, drain access cover, and British Telecom inspection cover

DID YOU KNOW?

The textures and patterns are not just decorative. If metal covers in the street were simply smooth and flat, they would get slippery in wet weather. Patterns and textures make non-slip surfaces!

Beer being delivered to a pub cellar

Making Rubbings

Make a collection of interesting rubbings. *But only on the pavement; never make a rubbing on the road!*

Choose a dry day and a time when the street is not busy. You will need large sheets of paper, thick crayons, an old brush, and some sticky tape.

Brush away loose grit from the cover's surface. Place a sheet of paper over it, and fix it down with sticky tape.

Rub evenly all over the paper with the whole side of the wax crayon. You will soon see the pattern emerging.

Make a collection of rubbings. Remember to write on each one where you made it. Some will be attractive enough to hang on the wall.

5

People at Work

What do you think the town would look like if all the sewers, gas pipes, electricity cables, telephone wires, drains, and water pipes were on the surface? It would be very messy and untidy, wouldn't it? Not to mention dangerous and unhygienic!

Usually all these things are hidden under the ground. That's all right until things go wrong, or new services need to be provided. Then someone has to sort out an underground problem.

Often, pipes and wires are fairly near the surface. Workers can get at them by lifting the inspection covers and lids which you have already noticed. Electricity and telephone wires have junction boxes which are often found in locked metal boxes on the pavement. This makes access easy.

However, some pipes lie much deeper, and the road or pavement needs to be dug up. Next time you see workers digging a hole or trench, have a closer look. *(But stay behind any barrier, and watch out for traffic.)*

Who is digging the hole and why? If you don't like to ask the workers, look for clues. Is there a van parked nearby? It may have a council or company name on it. If there are piles of new pipes beside the hole, are they narrow (for taking water into a building) or wide (for bringing waste water out)?

You might find all sorts of other clues by looking into holes and trenches. What sort of soil can you see? Is it the same all the way down? (See page 10 for more about soil changes.) Can you see old road surfaces or building foundations? Perhaps there are some very rusty old pipes. Sometimes, workers digging up roads find remains and objects from very long ago. Most town sites date back many hundreds of years.

How often is your street dug up? Look for different-coloured patches on the tarmac which show where holes have been filled in. Some street surfaces are littered with these patches. If you go over them on your bike they will give you a bumpy ride.

DID YOU KNOW?

One quarter of our water supply leaks from taps and pipes before it can be used. You may see an engineer walking along with a listening device. He uses it to hear whether there has been a leak in a pipe.

Some people claim to be able to detect underground water by walking along the surface holding a forked stick or divining rod. They call themselves water diviners. A certain movement of the rod indicates that there is water underground.

Tunnels under Towns

How many different sorts of tunnels have you been through? Railway tunnels, certainly. Road tunnels, probably. Can you think of other sorts of tunnel? What about a canal tunnel? If you have ever been on a canal boat holiday you will know canals are often tunnelled through hills. All these tunnels are passageways *through* obstructions.

But there are other types of tunnel, passageways *under* obstructions. Groups of buildings are often linked by underground tunnels. These let people or goods pass from one building to another without getting cold or wet outside, or having to cross a busy main road. Big hospitals may move their patients and equipment around through connecting passages underground.

Pedestrian subways are built under busy roads. These let people cross the road without having to dodge between traffic. Are there other uses for subways? See if you can spot any clues next time you use a subway crossing.

In some big cities the subways have little shops and kiosks, or even quite large shopping areas with cafés and toilets. The most obvious underground tunnel - if you live in a big city like Glasgow or Liverpool - is for underground trains.

Underground Mail Rail

The Post Office has its own London underground railway. Its 23 miles of track carries 10 million bags of mail per year.

The Victorians were great tunnel builders. They invented special machines for digging them. They constructed hundreds of miles of sewer tunnels, most of which are still in use. They also built tunnels to carry cast iron water pipes and gas pipes. These tunnels now carry things like cable TV wires and telephone wires.

Another of their engineering feats in tunnels involved hydraulic-powered water mains. This involved pumping water through tunnels under very high pressure. The pressure was great enough to be able to operate lifts, raise and lower cranes, and operate theatre safety curtains. The system is no longer used, but you can still find clues to its existence in some places. In London you might find manhole covers marked LHP.

Some towns have underground rivers which flow in pipes or along the sewer tunnels. See if you can find any evidence of this in your town.

Canals were often built through tunnels in hilly areas. These generally had no towpath, so the horses that pulled the narrow boats were taken over the surface. The workers on the boats had to lie on their backs and 'leg' the boat through the tunnel by 'walking' their feet along the walls or the roof.

Because tunnels under a town are used for so many different purposes, there are no maps that show all of them. Many have even been forgotten about.

Tunnels are sometimes used by criminals. They plan robberies with break-ins at basement level, and escape routes through sewer or other tunnels. Some famous prison escapes have been made by prisoners digging tunnels.

Discovering Geology

Most of us, when very young, have dug a hole hoping to find treasure or to reach the centre of the earth! We didn't get very far. But have you ever looked into a really deep hole and noticed anything about the soil? Was it the same as the surface earth, or did it change in colour or texture as the hole got deeper? Was there solid rock at the bottom?

The world's surface is covered with many layers of different soils and rocks. People who study these layers are called geologists. Next time you are walking past a building site, or see workers digging a deep hole, you could study some geology yourself.

Geologists have to be good detectives. Many of their clues are hidden under the ground. However, you can tell a lot about the geology of a town without digging holes.

Start by looking at the older buildings. Before the days of easy transport, buildings were usually made from nearby materials. This meant stone from local quarries, or bricks from local clay. This is one reason why towns and buildings in various parts of the country look very different.

Train journeys can provide more clues about geology. Trains can't go up steep hills, so the tracks often run through cuttings. If the sides of the cutting are vertical you will be able to see the separate layers of rock. Can you think of any other places where you could go to see this?

Geological Maps

If you are interested in the ground below, go to the local reference library. Ask to see geological maps of the area. A good detective will be able to find some clues on the map about why the town on the surface looks the way it does.

Limestone exposed in a railway cutting
A limestone building in Glastonbury

*A natural slate exposure
You would recognize it better as a slate roof*

Most bricks are made from clay, which is a soft, fine-grained rock. It contains different minerals in different parts of the country, so the baked bricks end up in a variety of colours, as you see below.

Can you spot the bands of flint in this chalk? Now can you spot the flints in the three walls below?

A sandstone building in Gwynedd (left) and a 'dressed' sandstone building in Sussex (right)

11

Working in the Bowels of the Earth

Can you imagine getting up on a lovely sunny morning and going to work under the ground? Thousands of people do it every day.

Miners may be the first people you think of. Many of them spend their whole working lives underground. Each day they go down the mine shaft in a very fast lift. The average depth in British coal mines is 450 metres. Then they walk (or catch a train, or ride on a conveyor belt) to their workplace; it could take an hour to reach it. At the coal-face the only light is from a torch fixed to their helmet.

Conditions for workers under the ground are often unpleasant. People who clean sewers have very messy, smelly jobs. They are called 'flushers' and you can read about them on page 22.

In the London Underground tunnels there are workers called 'fluffers' who clean the tracks. When the electric current is turned off at night, they scrape and rake fluff and dirt from the rails. Most of the fluff is human hair and dead skin cells. Sometimes they scrape off pieces the size of blankets! More than 2.5 million people travel on the London Underground every day. That makes a lot of litter, shed hair, skin cells and chewing gum to be removed. Yuck! Each cleaner fills nine or ten big plastic sacks each night.

There is also a tunnel-cleaning train which works like a giant vacuum cleaner. But nothing is as good as human labour for thorough cleaning of tunnels, rails and escalators.

A 'road-header' boring a tunnel through to the coal face of a Yorkshire mine

12

Many offices, department stores, libraries, hotels, hospitals, and other big buildings have staff who spend a lot of time working below ground. Often this is where the main storage or filing area is.

Banks often have their safes under the building, although bank workers normally go there only for a few minutes at a time.

Pubs have their cellars underground, where the beer can be kept cool. The beer barrels can be delivered through a trap door in the pavement outside. The barman connects the barrels to pipes leading to the bar above.

Hotels and restaurants often have their kitchens in the basement below ground. Can you imagine how hot and smelly it gets with the cookers and the vats of washing-up water?

Many public lavatories are underground. The attendants spend their working days in dingy, smelly places, and the visitors never stay for a chat. No wonder the attendants often look unhappy. Most new public loos are built on the surface.

In most towns you will find underground car parks where the attendants work in half light. Even in multi-storey car parks the pay kiosks are often under street level.

All in all, workers underground have rather unpleasant jobs and conditions, and very few of them are well paid.

A group of fluffers hard at work cleaning the tunnels of the underground railway

Uncovering the Clues

A very long time ago, there was nobody living in your town. In fact there was no town at all!

Can you imagine forests and fields where all the buildings are now? Most towns have grown from tiny farming settlements which may have started thousands of years ago.

In most places where people have lived, there are clues to the past. People who look for these clues are called archaeologists. They are excellent detectives when it comes to piecing together a picture of life in past times.

Most archaeological 'finds' are buried under the ground. This is not because people in the past deliberately buried everything. Over hundreds of years, dust and dirt blows around and covers things. Also buildings collapse or are pulled down, and new ones are built over the remains.

Archaeologists don't set out to look for hidden treasure like gold or silver. Instead they are looking for clues. Some of these can appear very boring or odd to us. One of the most exciting finds for an archaeologist is an old rubbish heap! It will be full of clues about what people grew on their land and ate. It may also contain broken pots and tools.

Archaeologists can also learn about the climate by studying seeds and pollen.

Your local museum will have samples of finds from your town such as pottery, coins, bones, and tools. There may also be reconstructions of life long ago. If your town has an archaeological society (ask at the library) you might also be able to visit some archaeologists at work.

Archaeologists are detectives working on the past. First they learn about the past by studying history. Then they do very careful searches and excavations which are called 'digs'.

Because they must not overlook the tiniest clue, digs are done incredibly slowly and carefully. Everything they find is recorded in detail. They take notes, make drawings and photographs, measure everything, then clean, store, and label their finds. Such accurate records can help them to reconstruct objects and even whole buildings.

Sadly, few pieces of evidence survive the years intact. Stone from old buildings is re-used. Hoards of treasure are stolen. Ancient burial grounds or settlements may be

Roman glass

Roman comb

flint arrowhead

Neolithic polished stone axe head

Roman coins

Bronze Age pot

ploughed up. Building foundations may destroy evidence. Clues have been removed or destroyed by unthinking curio seekers.

How about doing some archaeology yourself? You should never dig or use a metal detector in public places or historic sites. But if you have a garden, and the chief gardener at your home does not mind, you could do a little gentle digging there. Look for cooking pots, broken tools, old coins, bones, discarded toys, or crockery. In the days before dustmen called you'd be amazed at what people would bury in their gardens!

DID YOU KNOW?

The Romans invented underfloor central heating. They had concrete floors supported on pillars. Heat from a furnace flowed under the floors and into tunnels in the walls.

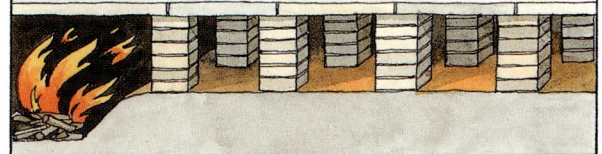

Living in the Past

Using evidence collected by archaeologists, a group of people constructed an Iron Age Farm at Butser Hill in Hampshire. They lived there for a short period, with only the sorts of tools, crops, farming methods, clothes and materials that settlers of 3,000 years ago had.

The walls of this hut are made of interwoven hazel or willow sticks called 'wattles'. The covering is a mixture of clay, straw, and even animal dung, called 'daub'; when dried out it becomes very hard.

Windproof fencing was made in the same way. These children are making a wattle and daub fence by picking up handfuls of daub and sloshing it on to the wattle hurdles. When they have finished the fence will be very strong and the children will be very dirty!

15

Cellars, Shelters and Dungeons

Cellars are exciting places, all dark and mysterious, full of spiders and ghosts and long-forgotten things! Modern houses don't have cellars. Why did old houses have them?

Under the ground, air stays at much the same temperature all the year round. The sun's heat and winter's frost only penetrate a few inches into the ground. Cellars stayed cool, so were good places to store food. (Refrigerators haven't been around for very long - ask your grandparents if their home had a fridge when they were young.)

Many big houses and restaurants still have wine cellars, and pubs use cellars to keep the beer barrels cool. There is another reason for cellars to store things which take up too much space elsewhere. Many older houses both big and small have coal cellars. The coal was delivered in sacks from a horse-drawn cart or lorry. In the pavement outside the house was a coal hole into the coal cellar. Few people in town have coal fires these days because they are messy, hard work, and the smoke causes pollution.

Many shops and offices have cellars or basements used for storage. Look for thick glass and metal covers in pavements. These let some daylight in.

The biggest underground store in your town is likely to be a reservoir full of water. If there is one in your area it will probably be marked on a street plan of the town. The water authorities might allow school parties to visit it.

There is a fortune in money hidden away under your town. But don't get too excited – it's probably all hidden away in bank vaults. In past times, however, before there were banks, people used to bury their coins and valuables beneath the floor of their house. Occasionally a forgotten hoard is discovered by accident, sometimes by children. Sadly, they can't keep it. It's called treasure trove, and belongs to the State.

During the air raids of the Second World War, many people used their cellars to shelter from the bombs. They made them as cosy as possible, with bunk beds and oil lamps. Others dug shelters in their gardens, and whole families would sleep the night there. Try to find an older person who remembers doing this and can tell you what it was like. The garden shelters were so strong that they were difficult to demolish when the war ended. Even now you occasionally see one of these old shelters.

There were also bigger shelters built in the street, for people caught in a raid while away from home. Schools in parts of the country that were regularly bombed had shelters in the playground. Pupils went to these during air raids, and even had lessons under the ground.

The government and army have special shelters called 'bunkers' in case of nuclear attack. They have thick lead doors and very thick walls. Some are several storeys deep, and contain enough food and water to keep people alive for weeks. Most of them are supposed to be top secret, but it's very hard to keep that sort of thing secret these days!

If you have visited a castle you might have seen the dungeons where unfortunate prisoners were kept. Can you imagine spending years in a cold dark dungeon? Centuries ago whole families, including children, sometimes had to live there. If father was a prisoner and they had no money there was seldom anywhere else for them to go.

This massive door opens to reveal the safe deposit deep underground in the vault underneath a bank

Living in the Dark

There is far more life below ground than there is above it. A vast animal world flourishes beneath our feet.

Black Ants live underground in tunnels and will come into houses looking for sweet foods like jam, sugar, or cake crumbs. If you look carefully you will find entrances to ants' nests. *Clue: tiny heaps of soil particles around a little hole.*

Rabbits and Badgers are very shy creatures, but if they burrow on railway embankments they will sometimes find their way on to waste ground or parks. *Clue: holes on embankments and around tree roots, and the animals' droppings.*

Earthworms burrow in the soil, pulling down leaves to close the opening. They eat their way through the soil, digesting the edible bits and passing the gritty bits out at the other end. *These 'worm casts' on the lawn are the clues to look for.*

A Spidery

Find a shoe box, or large jar, or a plastic food container. Cover it with glass or cling film. Punch small holes for air in the box or cling film. Furnish as shown in the picture. Then put in a spider - one only. Feed it on live flies and other small insects, and make sure there is always fresh water. Let the spider go after a few days, by putting it back where you found it.

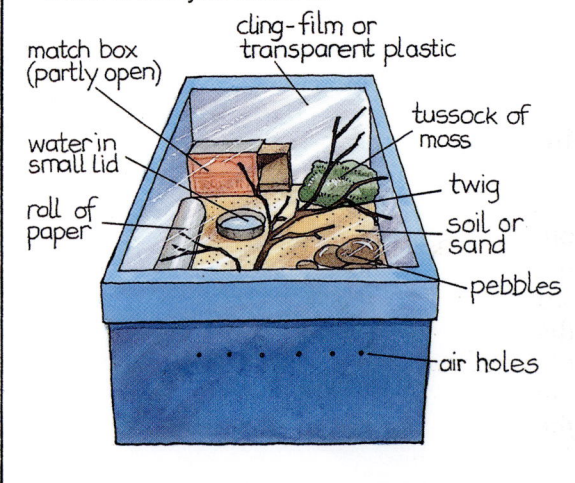

Spiders! There are more in your home than people (and many more in the garden). They hide away in daytime under ground or floor boards, or in cupboards. If you see a spider in the bath it's not because it has come up the waste pipe. It has fallen from above, and cannot climb up the slippery sides. *Clue: strands of web in corners, and screams from the bathroom!*

18

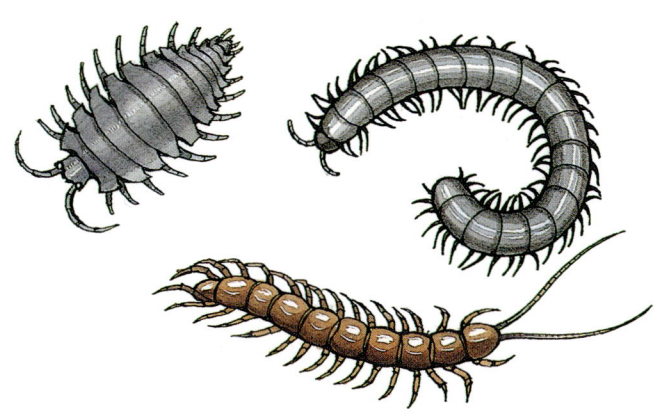

Moles spend their lives digging tunnels in the dark. They eat worms and other creatures, and surface only occasionally. *Clue: mole hills which are heaps of excavated soil from their tunnels.* Gardeners hate them!

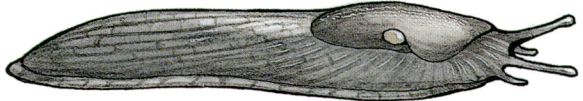

Woodlice, Centipedes and Millipedes are wriggly creatures which like to live in damp and dark places like cellars, cracks and crevices in the ground, and underneath pots and stones. They eat plant roots and decaying vegetation and are active at night. *Clue: look under pots and stones during the day, and with a torch at night.*

Slugs live in shady, damp places, often underground, and eat plant roots. At night they emerge to eat surface plants. *Clue: look for silvery slime trails, and shine a torch around plants at night.*

A Sluggery

Keep slugs as pets! You need a large jar with air holes in the lid. Put in a thick layer of moist soil, tussocks of grass, and a few stones for shelter. Feed the slugs on lettuce, cabbage, or slices of carrot. Remove stale food each day. After a week or two, look for eggs. Watch the young slugs developing. Keep the earth damp. After a while, let them free.

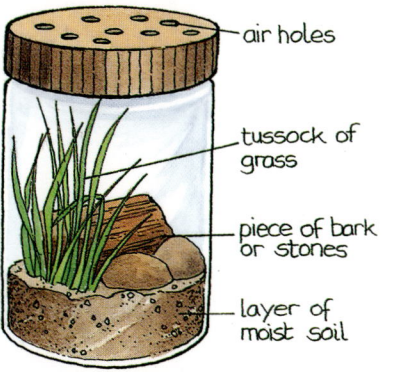

Brown Rats like to live in the sewers under our streets where there's plenty of food (they're not very fussy eaters!). They also live on canal and river banks in summer, and move into buildings in the winter. Rats are wonderful and clever creatures, but they carry disease. Sewer workers and pest control officers put down poison. Hundreds are killed but the survivors breed very fast. *Clue: look for droppings and mess around your compost heap. If you keep chickens, watch out for missing grain.*

Dead Bodies

Has it ever occurred to you that there are more bodies lying below your town than walking about on the surface?

Every town, however small, has at least one church with a graveyard. Underneath each gravestone there is not just one body. Graves do not last for ever, and at some time they have to make way for others. You have probably noticed that churchyards are a bit higher than the surrounding land.

Visiting an old graveyard can be very interesting. Gravestones can tell you quite a lot about the past. Look for family plots, the oldest grave, the youngest child. What do you notice about the length of life of women compared to men? Why do you think that so many children died so young?

Some of the stones can be works of art with fine lettering and carvings. They are not all single stone slabs. Some look like chests or tables, and are called table tombs. Old engravings of churches sometimes show people sitting round these, actually using them as tables. Don't copy them - these days it would be thought very disrespectful.

Bodies were often buried inside and underneath churches too. Have you ever been down into a church crypt? This is a large,

underground room beneath the main floor of the church. It was built to house tombs or early relics. In the days when pilgrims travelled all over the land, these crypts were regularly visited. These days they are often used for the general storage of church property, but they are still interesting places to see if the vicar will let you.

Crypts can also be found under big houses and stately homes. (Count Dracula was said to have lived in such a crypt!) Members of the family were buried here instead of in the local church.

Even some modern buildings have crypts, if they are built on the site of an old church. Crypts were so strongly built that they can provide the foundations of quite big buildings.

Stone and Brass Rubbings

You can make rubbings of gravestones in the same way as covers (see page 5). Inside some churches you may also find memorial 'brasses'. They are often set into the floor and covered by carpets. You can make very attractive rubbings of these, like the one below. But you *must* ask permission from the vicar first. His name and address will be shown somewhere near the entrance of the church. You can buy special crayons for brass rubbing from craft shops.

The Sewers

Sewers are underground channels which carry waste water from buildings and roads. When you flush the lavatory, or when rainwater flows along the gutters into the drains, it ends up in the sewers. The sewers link up with each other, running underground for miles and miles.

Every home, office, shop, and school in your town connects with the sewers.

Main sewers are big enough for a person to walk erect, but most of them are quite small. 'Man entry' sewers can be only three feet tall with the bottom foot full of muck!

Some sewers combine sewage with storm water from the surface drains. A sudden rainstorm can mean serious danger for the sewer workers, with a wall of water rushing down the tunnel. Sewer workers keep a careful eye on weather conditions.

In the old days, a surface worker had to warn the men underground of danger by lifting one of the heavy iron manhole covers a few inches and dropping it. The resulting noise echoed through the system and acted as a warning alarm. The workers had to make their way back to the surface manholes very quickly. Nowadays the use of two-way radios and closed circuit television makes the work safer.

People who clean the sewers are called 'flushers'. They usually work in teams of five, with a leader who is called a 'ganger'. The flushers main job is to shovel the sediment to prevent the sewers from blocking up. They also repair crumbling brickwork, and kill rats. In the larger tunnels they can lower water gates for a while, but they spend much of their time standing or wading in liquid sewage.

Dangerous gases can form, which cause the workers to wear breathing apparatus. Another hazard is the chemicals which factories flush down their drains. They are supposed to report this beforehand, but don't always remember to do so.

Some town councils organise tours of the sewers. Does the idea appeal to you? You could perhaps discuss it with your teacher. It would give you something to think about, next time you flush the lavatory.

Most of the sewer tunnels are a hundred years old. What did they do before they had sewers? Not long ago – 150 years or so – open drains ran through the streets of our cities, full of raw sewage! People had earth closets in their gardens or yards. Indoor or flushing toilets only became commonplace during this century.

Sewer Strangers

Sometimes strange wildlife turns up in the sewers. People have been known to get bored with pets like tropical fish, snakes, and even little crocodiles, and flush them down toilets and drains into the sewers!

Your own Model Town

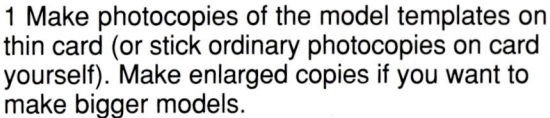
Assembling your Models

By making your own cardboard models you can create a street, neighbourhood, or whole town.

Most buildings are fairly simple shapes, so it can be quite easy to make tiny model versions.

The easiest way to start is to use these templates They must not be cut out of the book, but may be photocopied and coloured.

Try designing your own shapes for buildings too. It is easiest if you experiment with pieces of graph paper. This makes it simpler to get the folds in the right places and at the correct angles. Look at the examples of basic shapes and proportions below and use them as starting points.

1 Make photocopies of the model templates on thin card (or stick ordinary photocopies on card yourself). Make enlarged copies if you want to make bigger models.
2 Colour in your copy adding your own details.
3 Cut out your model. The red outlines printed in the book show you which lines to cut on your own sheet.
4 Now fold your model along the green lines shown in the book. It is best to score these first with the point of a pair of scissors.
5 Put a little glue on all the flaps, as shown on the template by blue shading.
(TIP: cut a thin strip of waste card and use it to apply and spread the glue).
6 Assemble the model as shown in the diagram.

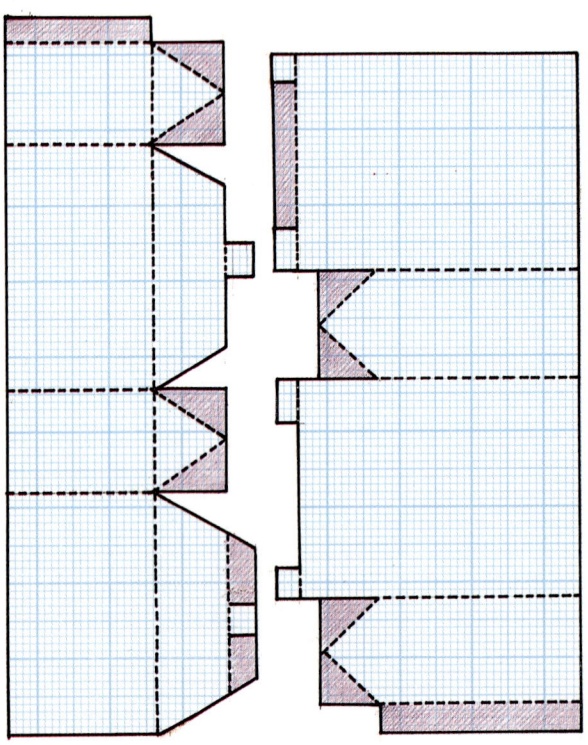

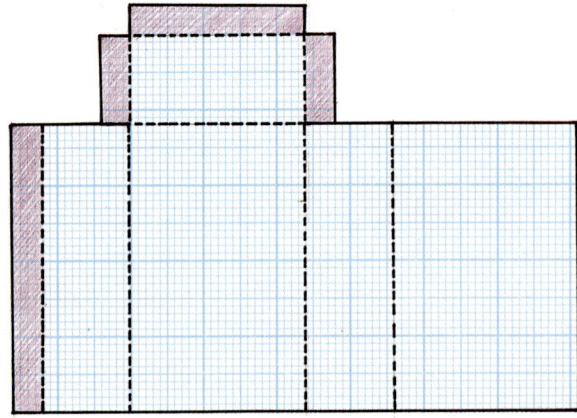

The Andersen Shelter
During the Second World War, people built air-raid shelters in their homes and gardens. The standard outdoor shelter was a hole in the ground, covered by concrete, corrugated iron, soil and grass.

The Graveyard... Have you constructed the model church using the template in the Urban Detective book 'History on your Doorstep'? Why not add a graveyard? Design some more tombstones of your own.

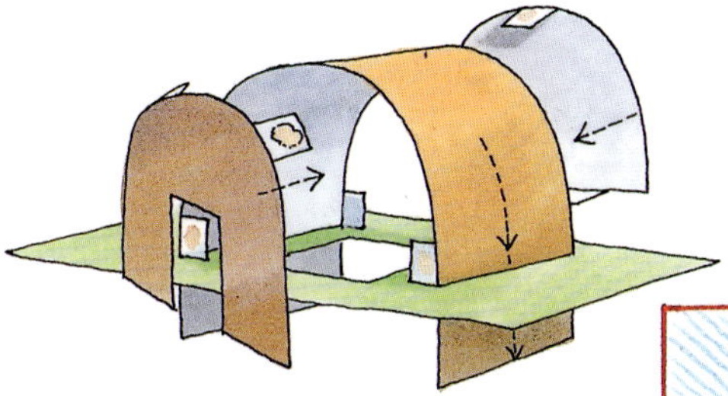

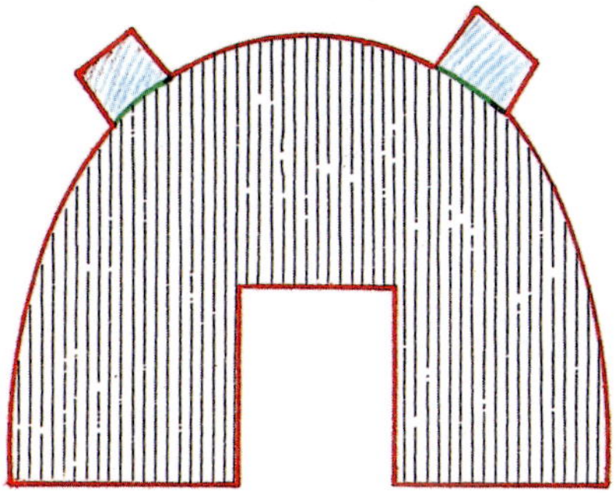

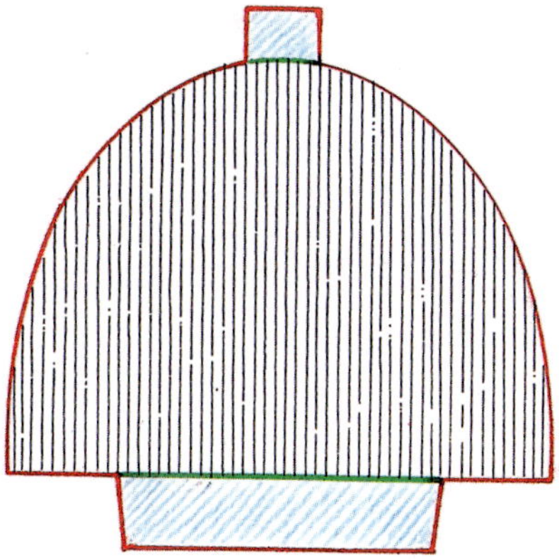

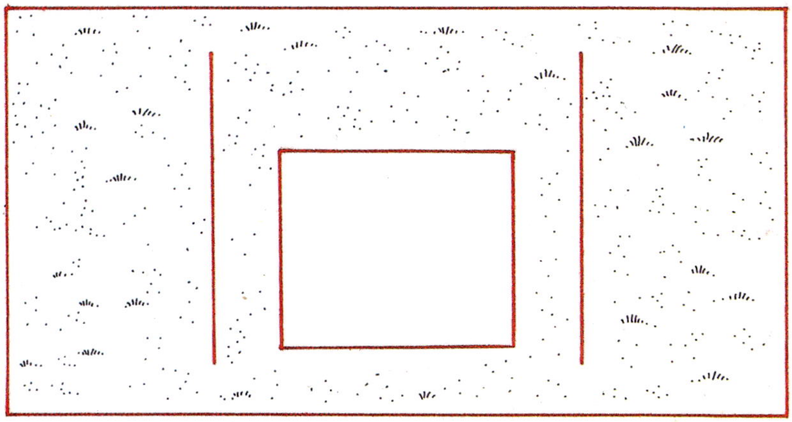

25

Books to Read

Coalhole Rubbings, Lily Goddard (Midas Books 1979)
London Under London, Richard Trench & Ellis Hillman (John Murray 1985)
All About Your Street, Stephen Scoffam (Cambridge University Press 1983)
Village Heritage, Miss Pinnell (Alan Sutton 1986)
The Young Scientist Book of Archaeology, Barbara Cork and Struan Reid (Usborne 1984)
The Young Archaeologist's Handbook, Lloyd and Jennifer Lang (Piccolo/Pan 1976)
Town and City Wildlife, Diana Shipp (Usborne Pocket Books 1981)
Church Memorial Brasses and Brass Rubbing, Leigh Chapman (Shire Publications 1987)
Visiting a Museum, Althea Braithwaite (Dinosaur Publications)
Map Reading & Local Studies in Colour, A P Fullagar & H E Virgo (Hodder and Stoughton 1967)
The Ordnance Survey Map Skills Book, Chris Warn (Arnold-Wheaton & Ordnance Survey 1980)
Plague and Disease, Richard Worsnop (Collins Educational 1987)
Farming in the Iron Age, Peter J Reynolds (Cambridge University Press 1976)

Acknowledgements

Photographs Bob Seago: 5 (bottom - courtesy Harveys Sussex Brewers), 10 (bottom), 17 (bottom right) 24 &25; Geoffrey Mead 10 &11; Southern Water Services Ltd: 22 & 23; Young Library: 12, 22; London Transport Museum: 13; British Telecom: 6; Midland Bank Group Archives: 19, The Post Office: 8; Butser Ancient Farm Queen Elizabeth Country Park Portsmouth: 15. All other photographs: Jane Launchbury & Lewis Cohen Urban Studies Centre at Brighton Polytechnic.
Research Assistance Denise Francis, Geoffrey Mead.

Selma Montford is the director of the Lewis Cohen Urban Studies Centre based at Brighton Polytechnic. It is an information and resource centre concerned with understanding the local environment.

There may be an Urban Studies Centre in your area; for a list of all Urban Studies Centres contact: the National Association for Urban Studies, Canterbury USC, 82 Alphege Lane, Canterbury, Kent CT1 2EB

Index

A number in **bold** type means there is a picture

A
Ancient settlements 14
Andersen shelter 25, **25**
Archaeological finds 14
Archaeologists 14

B
Badgers 18, **18**
Bank safes 13, **17**
Black ants 18, **18**
Brass rubbing 21, **21**
Brown rats 19, **19**
Building materials 10, **10**

C
Canals 9
Cellars 16
Centipedes 19, **19**
Churches 20, 21
Coal deliveries 4, **16**
Coal-hole covers 4, **4**
Count Dracula 21
Covers (in the ground) 4, **4**
Criminal tunnellers 9, **8, 9**
Crocodile 22

D
'Digs' 14
Divining rod 7, **7**
Drains 4, **4**
Dungeons 17

E
Earthworms 18, **18**
Electricity wires 6

F
Fence-making 15
Fluffers 12
Flushers 12, **13**, 22

G
Gardeners 10, 19
Gas pipes 9
Geological maps 10
Geologists 10

Glass covers **4**, 16
Gravestones 20, **21, 25**
Green Cross Code 2

H
Helpful adults 2
Highway Code 2
Holes in the road 7
Hotel and restaurant kitchens 13

I
Iron age farm 15, **15**

J
Junction boxes 6

L
Library 10

M
Manholes 9, 22
Millipedes 19
Miners 12
Moles 19, **19**
Museum 14

N
Narrow boats 9
Non-slip metal surfaces 5

P
Pipes and wires 6, 7
Post Office railway 8, **8**
Pub cellars 13
Pub deliveries 4, **5**
Public lavatories 13

R
Rabbits 18, **18**
Railway cuttings 10
Reservoir 16
Rock formation 10
Roman central heating 15
Rubbings 5, 21
Rubbish heap treasure 14

S
Safety tips 2
Second World War shelters 16, **25**
Sewers 9, 12, 19, 22, **23**
Sluggery 19, **19**
Slugs 19, **19**
Soil 10
Spiders 18, **18**
Spidery 18, **18**
Strangers 2

T
Tarmac repairs 7
Telephones 6, 9
Telephoning in an emergency 2
Textures on covers 5
Tours of sewers 22
Treasure trove 16
Tree root grille **4**
Tunnels 8, **12, 13**

U
Underground
  car parks 13
  rivers 9
  trains 8, 12
  workers 12, 13

V
Victorian tunnel-makers 9

W
Water diviners 7
Water pipes 7, 9
Water stopcock cover **4**
Wildlife in sewers 22, **22**
Wine cellars 16

27